READER'S DELIGHT

Biography of
Subhash Chandra Bose

READER'S DELIGHT

AN IMPRINT OF RAMESH PUBLISHING HOUSE

NEW DELHI

ISBN: 978-93-5012-251-8

Published by: Alok Kumar Gupta *for* Reader's Delight
(An Imprint of Ramesh Publishing House)

Admin. Office: 12-H, New Daryaganj Road, Opp. Officers' Mess,
New Delhi-110002 ☎ 23261567, 23275224, 23275124

Showroom: ● 2604, Balaji Market, Nai Sarak, Delhi-6 ☎ 23253720, 23282525
● 4457, Nai Sarak, Delhi-6 ☎ 23918938

E-Mail: info@rameshpublishinghouse.com
Website: www.rameshpublishinghouse.com

PREFACE

There are many things we know about the life of Netaji Subhash Chandra Bose. There are many mysteries about him as well which are not yet solved. The book covers all aspects of his life starting from his birth, family, education, his contribution in freedom struggle, philosophy and mystery disappearances and mystery over his death.

Bose was the elected President of the Congress and was the first to advocate complete independence of India. His entry, rising and exit from the congress are also discussed alongwith his sweet and sour relationship with Mahatma Gandhi and other leaders of Indian National Congress.

He was the first to organize an army within and outside India to wage war with the British. His relationship with Japan and Germany is also discussed in this book.

The book also consists some excerpts from his letters and speeches. It also describes how an introvert boy ultimately became the most dynamic and revolutionary leader of pre-independence India.

—**Publisher**

CONTENTS

INTRODUCTION

"Give me blood and I will give you freedom."

—Subhash Chandra Bose

Netaji Subhash Chandra Bose was the most visionary and fierce activist in the pre-independence era. He followed the path which no one else even could have dared of.

Under the leadership of Subhash Chandra Bose, an unparalleled example of the declaration of Independent Indian government with a cabinet and its own army, was seen in form of the Indian National Army. He literally made a military attack on British India and had confronted them till Imphal. With the help from Germany and active support from Japan, he shook the very foundation of the British Empire. He was acclaimed as a national hero and continues as a legend in Indian minds.

Subhash Chandra was born on January 23rd 1897 in Cuttack (in present day Orissa) as the ninth child among fourteen, of Janakinath Bose, an advocate, and Prabhavati Devi, a pious and God-fearing lady. A brilliant student, he topped the matriculation examination of Calcutta province and passed his B.A. in Philosophy from the Presidency College in Calcutta. He was strongly influenced by Swami Vivekananda's teachings and was known for his patriotic zeal as a student. He joined the Indian Civil Services in England as per his parent's wishes. This kept him a little away from the Indian Freedom Movement. He finished those examinations also, at the top of his class (4th rank), he did not complete his probation and returned to India, being deeply disturbed by the Jallianwala Bagh massacre. He came under the influence of Mahatma Gandhi and joined the Indian National Congress. Gandhiji directed him to work with Deshbandhu Chittaranjan Das, the Bengali leader whom Bose acknowledged as his political guru.

Due to his outspoken character for the British Government, he went to jail for around 11 times between 1920 and 1941 for periods varying between six months and three years. He was the leader of the youth wing of the Congress Party, in the forefront of the trade union movement in India and organized Service League, another wing of Congress. He was admired for his great skills in organizational development.

Subhash advocated complete freedom for India at the

earliest, whereas the Congress Committee wanted it in phases, through a Dominion status. Other younger leaders including Jawaharlal Nehru supported Bose and finally at the historic Lahore Congress convention, the Congress had to adopt Poorna Swaraj (complete freedom) as its motto. Bhagat Singh's martyrdom and the inability of the Congress leaders to save his life infuriated Bose and he started a movement opposing the Gandhi-Irvin Peace Pact. He was imprisoned and expelled from India. But defying the ban, he came back to India and was imprisoned again.

He was elected president of the Indian National Congress twice in 1937 and in 1939, the second time defeating Gandhiji's nominee. He brought a resolution to give the British six months to hand India over to the Indians, failing which there would be a revolt. There was much opposition to his rigid stand, and he resigned from the post of president and formed a progressive group known as the Forward Block (1939).

During the World War II, he was against rendering any kind of help to the British. He warned them so. The second World War broke out in September of 1939, and just as predicted by Bose, India was declared as a warring state (on behalf of the British) by the Governor General, without consulting Indian leaders. The Congress party was in power in seven major states and all state governments resigned in protest.

Subhash, now started a mass movement against utilizing Indian resources and men for the great war. To him, it made no sense to further bleed poor Indians for the sake of colonial and imperial nations. There was a tremendous response to his call and the British promptly imprisoned him. He took to a hunger-strike, and after his health deteriorated on the 11th day of fasting, he was freed and was placed under house arrest.

It was in 1941, that Bose suddenly disappeared. The authorities did not come to know for many days that he was not in the house in which he was being lodged. He traveled by foot, car and train and resurfaced in Kabul (now in Afghanistan), only to disappear once again. In November 1941, his broadcast from German radio sent shock waves amongst the British and electrified the Indian masses who realized that their leader was working on a master plan to free their motherland. It also gave fresh confidence to the revolutionaries in India who were challenging the British in many ways.

Germany assured Bose, military and other help to fight the British. Japan, by this time, had grown into another strong world power, occupying key colonies of Dutch, French, and British colonies in Asia. Bose had struck alliance with Germany and Japan. He rightly felt that his presence in the East would help his countrymen in freedom struggle and second phase of his saga began. It is told that he was last seen on land near Kiel canal in Germany, in the beginning of 1943. A most hazardous journey was undertaken by him under water, covering thousands of miles, crossing enemy territories. He was in the Atlantic, the Middle East, Madagascar and the Indian Ocean. Battles were being fought over land, in the air and there were mines in the sea. At one stage he traveled 400 miles in a rubber dingy to reach a Japanese submarine, which took him to Tokyo.

He was warmly received in Japan and was declared the head of the Indian army, which consisted of about 40,000 soldiers from Singapore and other eastern regions. Bose called it the Indian National Army (INA) and a government by the name "Azad Hind Government" was declared on the 21st of October 1943. INA freed the Andaman and Nicobar islands from the British and renamed them as Swaraj and Shaheed islands. Their Government started functioning there.

Bose wanted to free India from the Eastern front. He had taken care that Japanese interference was not present from any angle. Army leadership, administration and communications were managed by Indians only. Subhash Brigade, Azad Brigade and Gandhi Brigade were formed. INA marched through Burma (now Myanmar) and occupied Coxtown on the Indian Border. A touching scene ensued when the soldiers entered their 'free' motherland. Some lay down and kissed, some applied soil of mother earth on their foreheads, others wept. They were now inside India and were determined to drive out the British! Delhi Chalo (Let's march to Delhi) was the war cry.

The bombing of Hiroshima and Nagasaki changed the history of mankind. Japan had to surrender. Bose was in Singapore at that time and decided to go to Tokyo for his next course of action. Unfortunately, it is said, the plane he boarded crashed near Taipei and he died, in the hospital, of severe burns. He was just 48.

He was the man whom the Indians looked upon as their future leader. They never believed that he died in plane crash. They believe that he is still alive. No actual evidence of his death on that day has been authenticated and many committees were set up by the government of India to investigate the mystery of his presumed death. Whether or not he is alive, his contribution to India's freedom struggle will never be forgotten by us.

— ✳✳✳ —

FAMILY HISTORY

Subhash Chandra's mother, Prabhavati belonged to the family of Dutts of Hathkola, a northern suburb of Calcutta. The Dutts had attained eminence by their ability to adapt themselves to the new political order under the British.

Subhash with his family

His father, Janakinath joined the Cuttack Bar in 1885 and soon had a flourishing practice. He devoted his energies solely to his legal career, successively becoming government pleader and a public prosecutor. He later became Chairman of the Cuttack Municipality and in 1912 a member of the Bengal Legislative Council, collecting the title of *Rai Bahadur* on the way. By all contemporary standards, he was a successful man.

Although not directly involved in politics, Janakinath took an active interest in social and educational activities. A deeply religious man, he had a soft corner for the poor and the needy and his charities, especially to students, were extensive. During the Pujas, the chief festival in Bengal, he invariably visited his ancestral village Kedalia not merely to join in the celebrations but to extend help to the needy.

Janakinath's charitable disposition was fully shared by his wife Prabhavati. A woman of strong will, the task of bringing up her considerable family of fourteen children mainly devolved on her. Subhash was the ninth in order. Janakinath was a busy man. He was moreover reserved by temperament and he was glad to entrust the responsibility of looking after the children to his wife.

It was a typical middle-class household which steered clear both of the luxury and snobbery of the rich and the penury and greed of the poor. Subhash lacked nothing by way of creature-comforts but he craved for more parental contact which had to be shared by such a big brood. The children were in awe of their parents who, as was the usual practice in those days, refrained from making an undue exhibition of their affection. No wonder then that with his sensitive nature, Subhash felt like 'a thoroughly insignificant being.'

The emotional need for intimate contact with his parents was partially fulfilled by his nurse-cum-governess, Sarada, who called her ward 'Raja'.

Subhash thus grew up as an introspective, almost introverted child, but he was free of any egotism or pride.

— *** —

CHILDHOOD AND EDUCATION

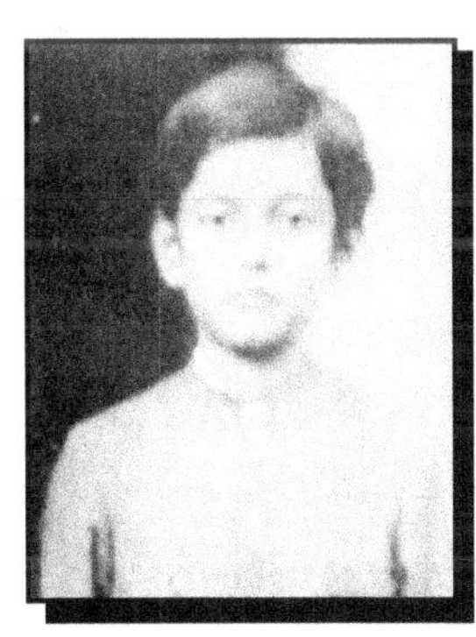

Young Subhash

In his childhood, Subhash Chandra was greatly influenced by his father and mother, particularly the latter from whom he derived his religious temperament. However, it would not be incorrect to say that even more than his parents, he was inspired by Beni Madhab Das, Headmaster of Ravenshaw Collegiate school, Cuttack. He almost 'adored' the Headmaster, and was strongly drawn to him.

Subhash passed the Matriculation examination, standing second in the Calcutta University, from the Ravenshaw Collegiate School. He entered the Presidency College, Calcutta, where he got involved in the "Oaten Incident". Prof. Oaten was assaulted by some students of the College who had been infuriated by the abusive language used by the Professor against India and Indians during one of his lectures. The high-spirited Subhash who had been in the black-list of the Principal for some time was held guilty as the prime mover in the incident, and was expelled from the College and rusticated from the University in 1916.

With the help of Sir Ashutosh Mukherjee he, however, got himself admitted to the Scottish Churches College in 1917 with a "no objection" certificate, and graduated in 1919 with a First class in Philosophy. He also joined the University Training Corps in 1917.

In 1919, Subhash's parents decided to send him to England, as they keenly desired that he should join the Indian Civil Service. The young man whose inner being had been set aflame by the incandescent spirit of Swami Vivekananda, and whose heart had already become the seat of spiritual aspiration and patriotic fervour, was in two minds about the objective set for him by his parents. He, however, finally submitted to their will, probably with mental reservations. In England, he appeared for the Indian Civil Service competitive examination in 1920, and came out fourth in order of merit. He also secured the "Cambridge Tripos" in Moral Sciences.

Subhash Chandra did not, however, complete the year of probation, which every successful candidate in the competitive examination was required to undergo. His mind had been deeply disturbed by grave developments at home after the heinous Jallianwala Bagh Massacre by General Dyer in 1919. He handed his resignation in April 1921 and returned to India to take part in the freedom struggle.

— *** —

MARRIAGE

In the second week of June 1934, Bose settled down in Vienna, since he had a contract from the publishing company 'Wishart' to write a book on the Indian struggle since 1920. In the course of looking for clerical help for preparing the manuscript, Subhash met a woman who brought about a dramatic change in his personal life. Until then, he had been immersed in the freedom struggle and had taken little

S.C. Bose with Emile Schenkl

interest in relationships with women. "So many did love me before," Subhash wrote later, "but I never looked at them."

On 24 June 1934, a petite and pretty young woman named Emilie Schenkl arrived to be interviewed for the clerical job. Born on December 26, 1910, to an Austrian Catholic family, she knew English, could take dictation in shorthand, and had competent typing skills. And what started as a working relationship, soon developed into a close personal bond.

It was on 26 December 1937 that Subhash secretly married Emilie. Despite the obvious anguish, they chose to keep their relationship and marriage a closely guarded secret. Emilie's explanation was simple. 'Country came first' for Subhash, and any public announcement at that stage would have caused unnecessary 'upheaval.'

Subhash and Emilie's daughter Anita was born on 29 November 1942 in Vienna. Subhash saw Anita in December only and they spent a quiet Christmas together in Vienna.

Their only daughter, Anita Bose Pfaff is an economist associated with the University of Augsburg, Germany.

— *** —

SUBHASH AND CONGRESS

Subhash handed his resignation from ICS in April 1921, and returned to India, reaching Bombay on July 16, 1921. He went straight to Mahatma Gandhi for guidance who directed him to Deshbandhu Chittaranjan Das, who had, in the

S.C. Bose with J.L. Nehru

meantime, flashed on the Indian Political firmament and become the uncrowned King of Bengal. From then on for a brief period of four years, till C.R. Das's death in1925, Deshabandhu was his political Guru.

Initially, Subhash Chandra Bose worked under the leadership of Chittaranjan Das, an active member of Congress in Calcutta. He regarded Chittaranjan Das as his political guru.

While Chittaranjan Das was busy in developing the national strategy, Subhash Chandra Bose played a major role in enlightening the students, youths and labors of Calcutta. He was eagerly waiting to see India, as an independent, federal and republic nation.

People began to recognize Subhash by his name and associated him with the freedom movement. He had emerged as a popular youth leader. He was admired for his great skills in organization development.

In 1927, after being released from prison, Bose became general secretary of the Congress party and worked with Jawaharlal Nehru for independence. Again Bose was arrested and jailed for civil disobedience; this time he emerged to become Mayor of Calcutta in 1930. During the mid-1930s, Bose traveled in Europe, visiting Indian students and European politicians, including Mussolini. He observed party organization and saw communism and fascism in action. By 1938, Bose had become a leader of national stature and agreed to accept nomination as Congress president.

During the Guwahati Session of the Congress, a difference in the opinion between the old and new members surfaced. The young leaders, as against the traditional leadership, wanted a "complete self-rule and without any compromise". The senior leaders were in favor of the "dominion status for India within the British rule".

— ✳✳✳ —

SUBHASH & NATIONAL POLITICS

The differences between moderate Gandhi and aggressive Subhash Chandra Bose were swelling. The state was so intense that Subhash Chandra

S.C. Bose with Gandhi

Bose had to contest and defeat Pattabhi Sitaramayya, a presidential candidate, nominated by Gandhiji himself. Though Bose had won the election but without any second thought he resigned from the party due to his differences with Gandhi. He, then formed the Forward Bloc in 1939.

He stood for unqualified Swaraj (self-governance), including the use of force against the British. This meant a confrontation with Mahatma Gandhi, who in fact opposed Bose's presidency, splitting the Indian National Congress party. Bose attempted to maintain unity, but Gandhi advised Bose to form his own cabinet. The rift also divided Bose and Nehru. Bose appeared at the 1939 Congress meeting on a stretcher. He was elected president again over Gandhi's preferred candidate Pattabhi Sitaramayya.

U. Muthuramalingam Thevar strongly supported Bose in the intra-Congress dispute. Thevar mobilised all south India votes for Bose. However, due to the manoeuvrings of the Gandhi-led clique in the Congress Working Committee, Bose found himself forced to resign from the Congress presidency. His uncompromising stand finally cut him off from the mainstream of Indian nationalism. Bose then organised the Forward Bloc on June 22, aimed at consolidating the political left, but its main strength was in his home state, Bengal. U Muthuramalingam Thevar, who was disillusioned by the official Congress leadership which had not revoked the Criminal Tribes Act (CTA), joined the Forward Bloc. When Bose visited Madurai on September 6, Thevar organised a massive rally as his reception.

Bose advocated the approach that the political instability of war-time Britain should be taken advantage of—rather than simply wait for the British to grant independence after the end of the war (which was the view of Gandhi, Jawaharlal Nehru and a section of the Congress leadership at the time). In this, he was influenced by the examples of Italian statesmen Giuseppe Garibaldi and Giuseppe Mazzini.

His correspondence reveals that despite his clear dislike for British subjugation, he was deeply impressed by their methodical and systematic approach and their steadfastly disciplinarian outlook towards life. In England, he exchanged ideas on the future of India with British Labour Party leaders and political thinkers like Lord Halifax,

George Lansbury, Clement Attlee, Arthur Greenwood, Harold Laski, J.B.S. Haldane, Ivor Jennings, G.D.H. Cole, Gilbert Murray and Sir Stafford Cripps. He came to believe that a free India needed socialist authoritarianism, on the lines of Turkey's Kemal Ataturk, for at least two decades. Bose was refused permission by the British authorities to meet Mr. Ataturk at Ankara for political reasons.

During his sojourn in England, only the Labour Party and Liberal politicians agreed to meet Bose when he tried to schedule appointments. Conservative Party officials refused to meet Bose or show him courtesy because he was a politician coming from a British colony. In the 1930s, leading figures in the Conservative Party had opposed even Dominion status for India. It was during the Labour Party government of 1945–1951, with Attlee as the Prime Minister, that India gained independence.

On the outbreak of war, Bose advocated a campaign of mass civil disobedience to protest against Viceroy Lord Linlithgow's decision to declare war on India's behalf without consulting the Congress leadership. Having failed to persuade Gandhi of the necessity of this, Bose organised mass protests in Calcutta calling for the 'Holwell Monument' commemorating the Black Hole of Calcutta, which then stood at the corner of Dalhousie Square, to be removed. He was put in jail by the British, but was released following a seven-day hunger strike. Bose's house in Calcutta was kept under surveillance by the CID, but their vigilance left a good deal to be desired. With two court cases pending, he felt the British would not let him leave the country before the end of the war.

Bose was not a person who would lie low and let the things pass by themselves. His burning desire to set India free made him think vigorously to be free from the house-arrest and go to other countries to gather their help to free India from the British.

— *** —

FORMATION OF INA

During the Second World War in September, 1939, Subhash Chandra Bose decided to initiate a mass movement. He started uniting people from all over

Formation of INA

the country. There was a tremendous response to his call and the British promptly imprisoned him. In jail, he refused to accept food for around two weeks. When his health condition deteriorated, fearing violent reactions across the country, the authority put him under house-arrest.

During his house-arrest, in January, 1941, Subhash made a planned escape. He first went to Gomoh in Bihar and from there he went on to Peshawar (now in Pakistan). He finally reached Germany and met Hitler. Bose stayed for almost three years in Berlin. In 1943, Bose left for south-east Asia and raised the army. The group was later named by Bose, as the Indian National Army (INA).

— *** —

ESCAPE FROM BRITISH INDIA

His burning desire to be free and make India free set the scene for Bose's escape to Germany, via Afghanistan and the Soviet Union. A few days before his escape, he sought solitude and

After Escape from British India

on this pretext avoided meeting British guards and grew a beard and on the night of his escape, he dressed as a Pathan to avoid being identified. Bose escaped from under British surveillance at his house in Calcutta on January 19, 1941, accompanied by his nephew Sisir K. Bose in a car that is now at display at his Calcutta home.

He journeyed to Peshawar with the help of the Abwehr, where he met Akbar Shah, Mohammed Shah and Bhagat Ram Talwar. Bose was taken to the home of Abad Khan, a trusted friend of Akbar Shah. On 26 January 1941, Bose began his journey to reach Russia through India's North West frontier with Afghanistan. For this reason, he enlisted the help of Mian Akbar Shah, then a Forward Bloc leader in the North-West Frontier Province. Shah had been out of India en route to the Soviet Union, and suggested a novel disguise for Bose to assume. Since Bose could not speak even one word of Pashto, it would make him an easy target of Pashto speakers working for the British. For this reason, Shah suggested Bose to act deaf and dumb, and let his beard grow to mimic those of the tribesmen. Bose's guide Bhagat Ram Talwar, unknown to him, was a Soviet agent.

Supporters of the Aga Khan III helped him across the border into Afghanistan where he met an Abwehr unit posing as a party of road construction engineers from the Organization Todt who then aided his passage across Afghanistan via Kabul to the border with Soviet Russia. After assuming the guise of a Pashtun insurance agent "Ziaudddin" to reach Afghanistan, Bose changed his guise and traveled to Moscow on the Italian passport of an Italian nobleman "Count Orlando Mazzotta". Once in Russia the NKVD transported Bose to Moscow where he hoped that Russia's traditional enmity to British rule in India would result in support for his plans for a popular rising in India. However, Bose found the Soviets' response disappointing and he rapidly passed over to the German Ambassador in Moscow, Count von der Schulenburg. He had Bose flown on to Berlin in a special courier aircraft at the beginning of April where he was to receive a more favorable hearing from Joachim von Ribbentrop and the Foreign Ministry officials at the Wilhelmstrasse. From Moscow, he reached Rome, and from there he traveled to Germany.

In Germany, he instituted the Special Bureau for India under Adam von Trott zu Solz, broadcasting on the German-sponsored Azad Hind Radio. He founded the Free India Center in Berlin, and created the Indian Legion (consisting of some 4500 soldiers) out of Indian prisoners of war who had previously fought for the British in North Africa prior to their capture by Axis forces. The Indian Legion was attached to the Wehrmacht, and later transferred to the Waffen SS. Its members swore the following allegiance to Hitler and Bose: "I swear by God this holy oath that I will obey the leader of the German race and state, Adolf Hitler, as the commander of the German armed forces in the fight for India, whose leader is Subhash Chandra Bose". This oath clearly abrogates control of the Indian legion to the German armed forces whilst stating Bose's overall leadership of India. He was also, however, prepared to envisage an invasion of India via the USSR by Nazi troops, spearheaded by the Azad Hind Legion; many have questioned his judgment here, as it seems unlikely that the Germans could have been easily persuaded to leave after such an invasion, which might also have resulted in an Axis victory in the War.

In all 3,000 Indian prisoners of war signed up for the Free India Legion. But instead of being delighted, Bose was worried. A left-wing admirer of Russia, he was devastated when Hitler's tanks rolled across the Soviet border. Matters were worsened by the fact that the now-retreating German army would be in no position to offer him help in driving the British from India. When he met Hitler in May 1942, his suspicions were confirmed, and he came to believe that the Nazi leader was more interested in using his men to win propaganda victories than military ones. So, in February 1943, Bose turned his back on his legionnaires and slipped secretly away aboard a submarine bound for Japan. This left the men, he had recruited, leaderless and demoralized in Germany.

Bose spent almost three years in Berlin, Germany from 1941 until 1943, during which he married Emilie Schenkl and a daughter Anita Bose Pfaff was born to them in 1942.

After being disillusioned that Germany could be of any help in liberating India, in 1943 he left for Japan. He traveled by the German submarine U-180 around the Cape of Good Hope to Imperial Japan (via Japanese submarine I-29). This was the only civilian transfer between two submarines of two different Navies in World War II.

He was warmly received in Japan and was declared the head of the Indian army, which consisted of about 40,000 soldiers from Singapore and other eastern regions. Bose called it the Indian National Army (INA) and a government by the name "Azad Hind Government" was declared on the 21st of October 1943. INA freed the Andaman and Nicobar islands from the British and renamed them as Swaraj and Shaheed islands. Their Government started functioning there.

— *** —

TAKING OVER LEADERSHIP OF AZAD HIND FAUZ

The Indian National Army (INA) was originally founded by Capt. Mohan Singh in Singapore in September 1942 with Japan's Indian POWs in the Far East. This was along the concept of—and with

S.C. Bose & Ras Behari Bose

support of—what was then known as the Indian Independence League, headed by expatriate nationalist leader Ras Behari Bose. The first INA was however disbanded in December 1942 after disagreements between the Hikari Kikan and Mohan Singh, who came to believe that the Japanese High Command was using the INA as a mere pawn and propaganda tool. Mohan Singh was taken into custody and the troops returned to the prisoner-of-war camp.

However, the idea of a liberation army was revived with the arrival of Subhash Chandra Bose in the Far East in 1943. In July, at a meeting in Singapore, Ras Behari

Bose handed over control of the organization to Subhash Chandra Bose. Bose was able to reorganise the fledgling army and organise massive support among the expatriate Indian population in south-east Asia, who lent their support by both enlisting in the Indian National Army, as well as financially in response to Bose's calls for sacrifice for the national cause. At its height, it consisted of some 85,000 regular troops, including a separate women's unit, the Rani of Jhansi Regiment (named after Rani Lakshmi Bai) headed by Capt. Lakshmi Swaminathan, which is considered as a first of its kind in Asia.

Even when faced with military reverses, Bose was able to maintain support for the Azad Hind movement. Spoken as a part of a motivational speech for the Indian National Army at a rally of Indians in Burma on July 4, 1944. Bose's most famous quote was "Give me blood, and I will give you freedom!" In this, he urged the people of India to join him in his fight against the British Raj. Spoken in Hindi, Bose's words were highly evocative. The troops of the INA were under the aegis of a provisional government, the Azad Hind Government, which came to produce its own currency, postage stamps, court and civil code, and was recognised by nine Axis states—Germany, Japan, Italy, the Independent State of Croatia, Wang Jingwei regime in Nanjing, China, a provisional government of Burma, Manchukuo and Japanese-controlled Philippines. Recent researches have shown that the USSR too had recognised the "Provisional Government of Free India".

Of those countries, five were authorities established under Axis occupation. This government participated in the Greater East Asia Conference as an observer in November 1943.

On the Indian mainland, an Indian Tricolour, modeled after that of the Indian National Congress, was raised for the first time in the town in Moirang, in Manipur, in north-eastern India. The towns of Kohima and Imphal were placed under siege by divisions of the Japanese, Burmese and the Gandhi and Nehru Brigades of INA during the attempted invasion of India, also known as Operation U-GO. However, Commonwealth forces held both positions and then counter-attacked, in the process inflicting serious losses on the besieging forces, which were then forced to retreat back into Burma.

When Japanese funding for the army diminished, Bose was forced to raise taxes on the Indian populations of Malaysia and Singapore. When the Japanese were defeated at the battles of Kohima and Imphal, the Provisional Government's aim of establishing a base in mainland India was lost forever. The INA was forced to pull back, along with the retreating Japanese army, and fought in key battles against the British Indian Army in its Burma campaign, notable in Meiktilla, Mandalay, Pegu, Nyangyu and Mount Popa. However, with the fall of Rangoon, Bose's government ceased to be an effective political entity. A large proportion of the INA troops surrendered under Lt. Col. Loganathan when Rangoon fell. The remaining troops retreated with Bose towards Malaya or made for Thailand. Japan's surrender at the end of the war also led to the eventual surrender of the Indian National Army, when the troops of the British Indian Army were repatriated to India and some tried for treason.

Earlier, in a speech broadcast by the Azad Hind Radio from Singapore on July 6, 1944, Bose addressed Mahatma Gandhi as the "Father of the Nation" and asked for his blessings and good wishes for the war, he was fighting. This was the first time that Mahatma Gandhi was referred to by this appellation.

— *** —

DISAPPERANCE AND MYSTERY OVER DEATH

The bombing of Hiroshima and Nagasaki changed the history of mankind. Japan had to surrender. Bose was in Singapore at that time and decided to go to Tokyo for his next course of action. Unfortunately, it is said, the plane he boarded crashed near Taipei and he died, in the hospital, of severe burns. He was just 48.

Bose is alleged to have died in a plane crash over Taihoku (Taipei), Taiwan, on 18 August 1945 while en route to Tokyo and possibly then the Soviet Union. The Imperial Japanese Army Air Force Bomber (Mitsubishi Ki-21), he was travelling on, had engine trouble and when it crashed Bose was badly burned, dying in a local hospital four hours later. His body was then cremated, and a Buddhist memorial service was held at Nishi Honganji Temple in Taihoku (Taipei). His ashes were taken to Japan and kept at the Renkoji Temple in Tokyo. This version of events is supported by the testimonies of a Captain Yoshida Taneyoshi, and a British spy known as "Agent 1189."

The absence of his body has led to many theories being put forward concerning his possible survival. One such claim is that Bose actually died later in Siberia, while in Soviet captivity. Several committees have been set up by the government of India to probe into this matter.

In May 1956, a four-man Indian team known as the Shah Nawaz Committee visited Japan to probe the circumstances of Bose's alleged death. However, the Indian government did not then request assistance from the government of Taiwan in the matter, citing their lack of diplomatic relations with Taiwan.

However, the Inquiry Commission under Justice Mukherjee, which investigated the Bose's disappearance mystery in the period 1999-2005, did approach the Taiwanese government, and obtained information from the Taiwan government that no plane carrying Bose had ever crashed in Taipei, and there was, in fact, no plane crash in Taiwan on 18 August 1945 as alleged. The Mukherjee Commission also received a report originating from the U.S. Department of State supporting the claim of the Taiwan Government that no such air crash took place during that time frame.

The Justice Mukherjee Commission of Inquiry submitted its report to the Indian government on November 8, 2005. The report was tabled in Parliament on May 17, 2006. The probe said in its report that as Bose did not die in the plane crash, and that the ashes at the Renkoji Temple (said to be of Bose's) are not his. However, the Indian Government rejected the findings of the Commission, though no reasons were cited.

Several documents which could perhaps provide lead to the disappearance of Bose have not been declassified by the Government of India, the reason cited being publication of these documents could sour India's relations with some other countries.

Several people believed that the Hindu sanyasi named Bhagwanji or 'Gumnami Baba', who lived in the house 'Ram Bhawan' in Faizabad, Uttar Pradesh at least until 1985, was Subhash Chandra Bose. There had been at least four known occasions when Gumnami Baba reportedly claimed he was Netaji Subhash Chandra Bose. The belongings of the sanyasi were taken into custody after his death, following a court order. These were later subjected to inspection by the Justice Mukherjee Commission of Inquiry.

The commission came down against this belief, in the absence of any "clinching evidence". The independent probe done by the Hindustan Times into the case, however provided hints that the monk was Bose himself. Some people believe that Gumnami Baba died on 16 September 1985, while some dispute this. The story of Gumnami Baba came to light on his death. It is alleged that he was cremated in the dead of night, just under the light of a motorcycle's headlamp, at Faizabad's popular picnic spot, on the bank of River Saraju, his face distorted by acid to protect his identity. Faizabad's Bengali community still pays homage at the memorial built at his cremation site on the anniversary of his birth. However, the life and activities of Baba remain a mystery even today.

Justice Manoj Kumar Mukherjee who probed into the disappearance of Netaji Subhash Chandra Bose stated in his report that the question of whether the sanyasi of Faizabad (Bhagwanji) was (or not) Bose "need not be answered" as there was no clinching evidence to prove it. However, he inadvertently stated in a documentary shoot that he believed Bhagwanji was none other than Bose. This revelation supports the view that Bose had not died in the plane crash in 1945, and was in fact in India after that.

Bose was posthumously awarded the Bharat Ratna, India's highest civilian award in 1992, but it was later withdrawn in response to a Supreme Court directive following a Public Interest Litigation filed in the Court against the "posthumous" nature of the award. The Award Committee could not give conclusive evidence on Bose's death and thus the "posthumous" award was invalidated.

Recently, Lok Sabha Secretariat, regarding the unresolved mystery surrounding the death of Netaji in Plane Crash in 1945, has corrected its recent book—*Honouring National Leaders : Statues and Portrais in Parliament Complex*—saying that "no irrefutable proof" existed of his demise in the accident.

— ✳✳✳ —

NETAJI'S SOCIAL PHILOSOPHY

The credentials of Subhash Chandra Bose as a socio-political thinker will be well traced on a careful study of his activities, letters, writings and speeches at different phases of the freedom struggle, indicating a process of evolution of his social, economic and political concepts connected with the development of his own mind  responding to the shifting environment in India and the World outside. The sum of his ideas and convictions constitutes his philosophy, though he was more of an actionist.

Views on Religion

It was under the influence of his parents that Subhash Chandra Bose developed a profoundly religious and spiritual frame of mind, and love for Hindu scriptures from his early life to the last days of his glorious career in the battlefields of South East Asia in 1945. His religious and spiritual propensity was further elevated and broadened in contact with the teachings of Ramakrishna Paramahansa and Vivekananda. He always had a small copy of Bhagavat

Gita in the breast pocket of his field uniform. He would plunge into deep meditation at dead hours of night even in the battlefields of South East Asia. While in Singapore, he used to drive to Ramakrishna Mission late at night, change into a priestly silk dhoti, shut himself up in the prayer room with rosary in hand and spent a couple of hours in meditation. He would display his deep devotion to God in the hours of sorrows and sufferings, weal and woe of his life.

Subhash Chandra Bose accepted Upanishadic concept of 'Tyaga' and imbibed the ideal of renunciation for self-realisation and became determined to work ceaselessly for the benefit of the country and its toiling masses.

Subhash Chandra Bose, being a secularist, had an attitude of impartiality towards all religions. According to him, the Government of Free India must have an absolutely neutral and impartial attitude towards all religions and leave it to the choice of every individual to profess or follow a particular religion of his faith; Religion is a private affair, it cannot be made an affair of the State.

Bose was of the firm opinion that economic issues cut across communal divisions and barriers. The problems of poverty and unemployment, of illiteracy and disease, of taxation and indebtedness affected the Hindus and Muslims and other sections of the people as a whole.

For Subhash, there were no religious or provincial differences. Hindu, Muslim and Sikh soldiers in the Indian

National Army were made to realise that they were sons of the same motherland.

Bose writes in his autobiography, "In fact I cannot remember even to have looked upon Muslims as different from ourselves in any way except that they go to pray in Mosque."

In his public speech Subhash advocated emphatically the abolition of caste system in India and introduced observance of Anti-touchability Week from April 6th to 13th. He supported intercaste marriage in India. As a true disciple of Swami Vivekananda, Bose understood that the progress of India would be possible with uplift of the down-trodden and the so-called untouchables who constitute the very essence of our society.

All Indians living in South East Asia were united in the Indian National Army irrespective of caste, race, sex and creed under the stirring leadership of Subhash Chandra Bose in a spirit of Unity, Faith and Sacrifice with the sole objective of emancipation of Mother India.

Views on Women

Subhash Chandra Bose imbibed the ideals of his political mentor, Deshabandhu Chittaranjan Das and spiritual mentor, Swami Vivekananda in regard to female education and female emancipation. Bose wanted that women should be given a very elevated position in the family and society, and believed in female emancipation in the true sense of the term and in liberating women from all shackles and artificial disabilities—social, economic and political. According to him, in the Free India, there must not be any discrimination on ground of caste, race, sex, creed or wealth.

Subhash Chandra Bose rightly diagnosed that illiteracy and economic dependence were the root cause of serfdom of women. He spoke in favour of all-round education for women. He was a supporter of widow remarriage and abolition of Purdah system.

Subhash Chandra Bose in the later years commended the glorified role played by Indian women in the freedom movement.

Views on Education

According to Subhash Chandra Bose, education was necessary for character building and all round development of human life. Education brings forth the internal discipline in the form of control or regulation of mind and thoughts, which in its turn produces external discipline of control of action or deeds.

Education helps to awaken the mind which is the store-house of all knowledge. Education would boost of character, morale, varility and freedom of man. The problem of illiteracy was a fundamental problem to him.

Bose realised that education is a great force in bringing about a sense of national unity and solidarity.

— ✱✱✱ —

NETAJI'S ECONOMIC PHILOSOPHY

Subhash Chandra Bose spelt out his ideas about economic planning and industrialisation of Free India, "The very first thing which our future National Government will have to do, would be to set up a Commission for drawing up a comprehensive plan of reconstruction." Bose wanted that on the advise of the National Planning Commission, State would adopt a comprehensive scheme for gradually socializing our entire agricultural and industrial system in the spheres of both production and distribution. He also spoke about abolition of landlordism and liquidation of agricultural indebtedness.

According to Subhash, liberty broadly signified political, economic and social freedom. For him, economic freedom was the essence of social and political freedom.

He was very much in favour of large-scale industries but at the same time, he never lost sight of cottage and small industries in an under-developed country like India. He desired economic reconstruction and industrialisation on modern scientific and technological methods.

— *** —

NETAJI'S POLITICAL PHILOSOPHY

The political philosophy of Subhash Chandra Bose requires an enunciation and analysis from the angles of his spiritualistic, nationalistic, secularistic, democratic and socialistic views.

Spiritualistic Views

A spiritual approach of life was originally initiated under the influence of his deeply religious parents. Subsequently, his searching mind, right in his school days could explore out the meaning, significance and objectives of human life when he came in contact with the teachings, writings and philosophy of Ramakrishna Paramahansa, Swami Vivekananda and Sri Aurobindo Ghosh.

Nationalistic Views

Subhash Chandra Bose's father was a government pleader and Public Prosecutor and became a member of the Bengal Legislative Council and earned the title of Rai Bahadur, but he resigned from the said post and renounced the title of Rai Bahadur as a protest against the repressive policies of the British Government. Moreover, he was a regular visitor to the annual sessions of the Indian National Congress and a staunch supporter of Swadeshi. Thus Subhash inherited the spirit of nationalism from his father.

Subhash's nationalistic zeal was further hightened under the influence of Swami Vivekananda.

Secularistic Views

Subhash's philosophy of nationalism acquired a spiritual tenor under the influence of his parents, Ramakrishna Paramahansa, Vivekananda and Aurobindo Ghosh. He was secular in approach to spiritualism or religion.

Subhash was brought up in a liberal and secular environment of his family which helped him to acquire a broad and non-sectarian outlook towards people of all religions. The synthesis of various religious creeds thus achieved. Subhash's secularism originated from his firm faith in a philosophy of synthesis of Indian culture and civilization. In his Azad Hind Government and Army he had achieved miraculous success in bringing about a wonderful sense of unity among the Muslims, Hindus and Sikhs.

Socialistic Views

In his Free India, Subhash Chandra Bose had the aim of creating an egalitarian society in which all members would enjoy almost equal economic benefits and social status, and there would not be any distinction between man and man on account of accident of birth, parentage, caste and creed.

He said, "Free India will not be a land of capitalists, landlords and castes. Free India will be a social and political democracy .... a reign of perfect equality, social, economic and political" shall prevail in Free India.

Democratic Views

Subhash Chandra Bose developed an ethical approach to life based on sacrifice, renunciation, self-abnegation and self-sacrifice which is in a way the core of a democratic way of life.

Subhash valued freedom of thought and action. He meant a State, "It will work as an organ or as the servant of the masses ... the servant of the people."

His Democratic theory emphasises on the common man as the agent of change, evolution and progress.

National Defence View

Subhash Chandra Bose said, "The moment India is free, the most important problem will be the organising of our national defence in order to safeguard our freedom in the future."

— ✳✳✳ —

NETAJI'S LETTERS AND SPEECHES

Subhash, about "The Oaten Affair" wrote in his autobiography, "I reviewed the events of the last few months. My educational career was at an end and my future was dark and uncertain. But I was not sorry, there was not a trace of regret in my mind for what I had done. I had rather, a feeling of supreme satisfaction, of joy that I had done the right thing, that I had stood up for our honour and self-respect and had sacrificed myself for a noble cause. What is life without renunciation? I told myself. And I went to sleep."

He wrote to his elder brother Sarat Chandra on 22 September 1920, soon after the result of I.C.S. was declared: "After all, is service to be the be-all and end-all of my life? The civil service can bring one all kinds of worldly comfort, but are not these acquisitions made at the expense of one's soul? I think it is hypocrisy to maintain that the highest ideals of one's life are compatible with subordination to the conditions of service which an I.C.S. man has got to accept. National and spiritual aspirations are not compatible with obedience to civil service conditions."

He wrote to his brother, Sarat Chandra, from jail on being offered amnesty for permanent exile from India, "I have, on this occasion tried to anticipate the worst that may befall me if I do not accept the offer of government, but I have not been able to persuade myself that a permanent exile from the land of my birth would be better than life in a jail leading to the sepulchre. I believe 'The paths of glory lead but to the grave'."

The speech Bose delivered as Chairman of the Reception Committee of the Youth Congress in Calcutta in December 1928.

> The actual effect of the propaganda carried on by the Sabarmati (i.e., the Gandhian) school of thought is to create a feeling and impression that modernism is bad, large-scale production is an evil, wants should not be increased and the standard of living should not be raised, that we must endeavour to the best of our ability, to go 'back to the days of the bullockcart' and that the soul is so important that physical culture and military training can well be ignored.

> It is the passivism, not philosophic but actual, inculcated by these schools of thought against which I protest. In this holy land of ours, ashrams are not new institutions and ascetics and yogis are not novel phenomena. They have held and will continue to hold an honoured place in society. But it is not their lead that we shall have to follow if we are to create a new India at once—free, happy and great.

In India, today we want a philosophy of activism. We must be inspired by robust optimism. We have to live in the present and to adapt ourselves to modern conditions.

Everything seemed to be going smoothly at the session of Congress when, Bose stood up and moved an amendment and put a straight question to the delegates:

In the main resolution you have given twelve months' time to the British government. Can you lay your hands on your hearts and say that there is any reasonable chance of getting Dominion Status within this period? Pandit Motilal Nehru has made it clear in his speech that he does not think so. Then why should we lower the flag for these twelve months? Why not say we have lost the last vestige of faith in the British government and that we are going to take a bold stand?

He always asked the youngmen and women to think for themselves.

"On occasions," he told his youthful audience in Nagpur, "you will have to take the responsibility of creating public opinion or of stemming the tide of public feeling. If you want to solve the fundamental problems of public life, you will have to look miles ahead of your contemporaries. The mass mind is often unable to cut itself off from present-day moorings and visualise the future. It is not improbable that the mass mind will refuse to accept your prescription." "On such an occasion", Bose continued, "you must summon courage to stand out alone and friendless, in the presence of the cross as it were and fight the rest of the world. One who desires to swim with the tide of popular approbation on all occasions may become the hero of the hour, but he cannot live in history .... For the most unselfish actions, we should be prepared to get abuse and vilifications; from our closest friends, we should be prepared for unwarranted hostility."

During his routine inspection visit to the prison, the Chief Presidency Magistrate of Madras asked Bose whether he was comfortable. Promptly came Bose's retort: "You should feel ashamed of yourself and your government to keep me a prisoner without any charge or trial! Don't you see that it is sheer mockery to ask such a prisoner if he is comfortable? Why don't you put yourself in this position and then get the answer yourself?

In one of his letters, he expatiated on the need for a guru to make one realise one's duty and proper sphere of work.

His famous slogans were "Give me blood and I will give you freedom", "Dilli Chalo". This was the call he used to give the INA armies to motivate them. "Jai Hind", or, "Glory to India!" was another slogan used by him and later adopted by the Government of India and the Indian Armed Forces. INA also used the slogan "Inquilab Zindabad", which was coined by Maulana Hasrat Mohani.

— *** —

SUBHASH—A REVOLUTIONARY FREEDOM FIGHTER

Subhash Chandra Bose felt that young militant groups could be moulded into a military arm of the freedom movement and used to further the cause. Gandhiji opposed this ideology because it directly conflicted with his policy of Ahimsa (non-violence). The British Government in India perceived Subhash as a potential source of danger and had arrested him without any charge on October 25, 1924. He was sent to Alipore Jail, Calcutta (now Kolkata), and on January 25, 1925 transferred to Mandalay, Burma (now Myanmar). He was released from Mandalay in May, 1927 due to his ill health. Upon returning to Calcutta, Subhash was elected president of the Bengal Congress Committee on October 27, 1927.

Subhash was one of the few politicians who sought and worked towards Hindu-Muslim unity on the basis of respect of each community's rights. He, being a man of ideals, believed in independence from the social evil of religious discord.

— ✳✳✳ —

SUBHASH—A PROVEN METTLE

Subhash Chandra first proved his mettle in a thorough manner in which he worked for the total boycott of the Prince of Wales in Calcutta in 1921; subsequently his capacity for organisation and executive ability were amply demostrated in the discharge of his duties as Chief Executive Officer of the Calcutta Corporation during the mayoralty of C.R. Das. The Government, however, soon clamped him behind the bars in distant Mandalay on the trumped-up charge that he was actively associated with the terrorists of Bengal.

However, after three years of detention without trial under the obnoxious Regulation III of 1818, he was released in 1927 on medical ground, and soon began to take an active part in political life despite his shattered health. He was elevated President of the Bengal Provincial Congress Committee. He devoted much of his time and attention to the organisation of the youth and to the Trade Union movement as well.

— *** —

SUBHASH AS A SOCIAL WORKER

His spiritual quest would be more rapidly fulfilled, Subhash thought, if he found a guru in the true Indian tradition. He came across a ninety-year-old sanyasi whose precepts he diligently put into practice, but this failed to give him mental peace. Subhash therefore had to return to Vivekananda's gospel of social service. With like-minded friends, he started visiting nearby villages to render the rural community help.

Bose's superb ability as a social worker was demonstrated when he was deputed by the Bengal Provincial Congress Committee to organise relief work in the districts of Bogra, Rajashahi, Patna, Dinajpur and Rangpur inundated by floods of unprecedented magnitude in 1922. Food crops were destroyed, hundreds of houses reduced to rubble and innumerable head of cattle swept away. Bose organised a band of volunteers and went with them to the affected areas to distribute food, agricultural implements and house-repairing material. Bose and his devoted volunteers worked day and night to put the destitutes on their feet. The relief organisation was a unique success and earned, for the Congress and Bose personally, the thanks of Lord Lytton, Governor of Bengal.

— *** —

IMPACT OF SWAMI VIVEKANAND ON SUBHASH

It was the teachings of Swami Vivekananda, the famous disciple of Ramakrishna Paramhansa, which helped to resolve Subhash's mental crisis. He pored over Vivekananda's books day and night and they provided a satisfactory solution to the problems which were worrying his mind. "Seek your own salvation in the welfare of humanity", was the essence of Vivekananda's teachings. This fresh interpretation of India's ancient scriptures appealed immensely to Subhash who sought to inculcate it among his circle of friends.

His craving for higher values and spiritual uplift was reflected in his letters to his mother in 1912-13. They reveal the mystic strain which remained with Bose throughout his life. "Without realisation and divine revelation life is worthless", he wrote in one letter and added, "worship, meditation, prayer, contemplation, etc. that man engages in, have only one aim — realisation of the Divine. If this purpose is not fulfilled, all else is in vain. One who has tasted his heavenly bliss once, will never turn to the sinful material world."

— ✳✳✳ —

SUBHASH AS A PERSON, BROTHER & HUSBAND

As a Person

Netaji Subhash Chandra Bose was tall, well above the average and was somewhat predisposed to obesity. Subhash Chandra Bose's chubby face with its cherubic smile concealed a granite core of will. Gentle and affectionate in disposition, he could be very firm, even relentless whenever occasion demanded. To know him was to love him.

As a Brother

To his elder brother Sarat Chandra Bose, a renowned advocate and a political leader in his own right, Subhash was deeply attached, and it was Sarat Chandra who financially helped him, in the early years of his career, and backed him politically during the vicissitudes of his turbulent and meteoric career.

As a Husband to his wife

In a letter, Subhash wrote to his wife, "You are the first woman I have loved." "God grant that you may also be the last."

— *** —

IMPORTANT EVENTS IN NETAJI'S LIFE

1897: Born to Sri Janaki Nath Bose and Prabhavati Devi in Cuttack, Orissa.

1913: Stood second in the School leaving examination and took admission in Presidency college, Calcutta.

1915: Passed Intermediate examination in first division.

1916: Charged for misbehaving with British Professor, rusticated from Presidency college.

1917: Got admitted in Scottish Church college in Philosophy Honours.

1919: Got first class in Philosophy Honours and left for England for ICS examination.

1920: Passed the then ICS examination in London with highest marks in English.

1921: He got the prestigious Tripos degree of Cambridge University.

Resigned from his ICS job and came back to India in the same year. Formed South Calcutta Sevak Samity. Was arrested in the end of 1921 for anti-British movement.

1922: Released from jail on August 1. Joined Swarajya Dal under the leadership of Deshbandhu Chittaranjan Das in Gaya Congress.

1923: Elected President of All India Youth Congress; elected Secretary of Bengal State Congress and Editor of the paper 'Forward', founded by Deshabandhu.

1924: Swarajya Dal won Calcutta Municipality election. Deshabandhu elected Mayor of Calcutta and Subhash Chandra became CEO. Arrested again in October by the British Government.

1924-27: Spent nearly three years in the Burma jail; released in May.

1927: Elected General Secretary of All India Congress Committee.

1928: Formed the Volunteer Organization in the Calcutta summit of Indian Congress and elected as the General Officer in Command.

1929: Addressed the Lahore summit of Indian Congress and proposed for a parallel Government in India.

1930: Jailed in January again; elected Mayor of Calcutta Corporation from jail.

1931: Elected President of INTUC in Calcutta meeting.

1933-36: Met reputed personalities like Mussolini in Italy, Felder in Germany, D. Valera in Ireland and Roma Rolland in France.

1936: Returned to India in April; arrested in Bombay.

1936- Released in March and started for Europe;
37: published 'Indian Struggle'.

1938: Elected President of Indian Congress; made the historic speech in Haripura convention; formed National Planning Commission. Rabindra Nath Tagore felicitated Subhash Chandra in Shanti-niketan.

1939: Re-elected President of Indian Congress; resigned and formed the new organization Forward Bloc.

1940: Arrested and started fasting in the jail; released from the jail.

1941: Left home and disappeared; reached Kabul and then left for Moscow; met Hitler in Berlin.

1942: Made the historic speech on air from Germany; formed Indian Legion and expanded its activities.

1943: Started for Japan by submarine; reached Tokyo and delivered the speech on air in Tokyo; convened the meeting of South East Asian Indian Independence League.

Formed the Azad Hind Government on October 21; visited Andaman islands in December.

1944: The Azad Hind Fauz approached the Arakan front; war breaks out near Imphal and Azad Hind Fauz took control of Kohima-Imphal; rejected the peace proposal of British Government through a speech on air; reached Tokyo to discuss with Japanese Government; addressed a massive public meeting in Kualalampur.

1945: Delivered the speech on air from Sonan Radio; started for Bangkok.

Laid foundation stone for Martyrs' statues at Sonan; Hiroshima and Nagasaki destroyed by atom bomb by the Americans; Japan surrenders; Subhash left Saigon to implement his future plans. Mysteriously disappeared and alleged to have died in a plane crash over Taipei, Taiwan on 18 August, 1945.